Relationship Workbook for Couples

Build Trust, Improve Communication Skills, Boost Emotional Intimacy and Grow a Deeper Connection in Your Marriage With Mindful Habits And Counseling Therapy Techniques

Christian Silverman

LEGAL DISCLAIMER

Table of Contents

4

Introduction

Relationships are the backbone of our functioning society. There are numerous different types of relationships out there, ranging from romantic relationships to familiar relationships. The term 'relationship' is one that is frequently used in the world of psychology and in multiple languages all over the world. Relationships are defined as 'the way in which two or more concepts, objects, or people are connected, or the state of connected.' In this book, we will be studying the relationships between people and how we can improve them using communication.

When people think 'relationship,' they always automatically think about the romantic kind. Although that is the one that jumps to mind when we hear that word, there are numerous different types of relationships. Even within romantic relationships alone, there are a variety of different kinds with more and more evolving in our modern world today. We can pretty much sum up all relationships into just four types (romantic, familial, friendships, professional), but there are actually hundreds of different types of relationships if we wanted to get really specific.

If you're reading this book, you are likely someone that is looking to either improve relationships or find new relationships that are unhealthy. Did you know that nearly 2 million high school students in the U.S. experience physical abuse from a dating partner in one year? Or that one in three adolescents are victims of physical, verbal, or sexual abuse? Relationship building skills are extremely important not only to leave unhealthy situations but to be able to detect unhealthy behaviors to prevent getting involved with someone that may be exhibiting abusive behaviors.

When it comes to the topic of relationships, most people don't actually know what they're doing. Most people feel exhilarated during the early stages of a romantic relationship, but as they get back into their regular daily routine, their personal baggage begins to reveal itself and people often find themselves in the midst of escalating conflict, hurt feelings, emotional withdrawal, insufficient coping techniques or just plain boredom. There is absolutely no denying that maintain a healthy and happy relationship is a difficult task.

Luckily for us, there is a growing field of research focused on the area of relationships that provide science-based solutions and guidance into building healthy habits to foster the happiest relationships. Relationships are built not only love, but the science behind it as well. We will be learning about the fundamental lessons that are simply but difficult to master at the same time regarding the basics of relationships and how communication can help improve them.

What Does a Healthy Relationship Mean?

In order to learn about improving our own relationships into healthy ones, we first have to understand what a healthy relationship means. Although different types of relationships have different standards of healthiness, they all follow a similar guideline. To make things simple, we will focus on what a healthy romantic relationship is like within this subchapter.

To have a healthy romantic relationship, the couple needs to have three things; healthy communication, healthy boundaries and healthy relationship boosters. Honest, open, and safe communication is crucial when it comes to having a healthy relationship. The first step into building one is to make sure both people understand each other's needs and expectations. The two people have to be on the same page; this is very important. In order for two people to be on the same page, they must always be communicating. Most healthy relationships follow these five components:

- **Speaking up:** When a relationship is healthy, the people in the relationship are comfortable with talking about a problem rather than holding it in.

- **Respect:** In a healthy relationship, each person values the other's wishes and feelings. They let each other know when they are making an effort to keep their best interests in mind. Having mutual respect is an essential part of having a healthy relationship.
- **Compromise:** Arguments or disagreements are normal in healthy relationships; this means that learning to compromise when two people disagree on something is important. People in healthy relationships solve a conflict in a healthy way using compromises so that both parties are satisfied.
- **Support:** Healthy relationships are all about supporting each other and not putting each other down. Two people in a relationship should always be offering encouragement and reassurance to one another. It is also important to let each other know when one needs support.
- **Privacy:** Healthy relationships require space and personal time for both parties. Just because two people are in a relationship doesn't mean that they constantly need to be together or to share everything together.

Relationships that have healthy boundaries are more secure compared to the ones that don't. Creating boundaries together as a couple means that both people will have a better understanding of what type of relationship they have together. Keep in mind that boundaries are not meant to make one or both people feel like they are 'walking on eggshells.' Having boundaries also does not mean that there is distrust or secrecy. Instead, it is simply a way to express the things that make you comfortable or uncomfortable or what you would like to happen or not happen within the relationship. Healthy boundaries should not restrict these following abilities:

- Participating in hobbies and activities that you enjoy without your partner.
- Going out with friends or other people without your partner.
- Not needing to share passwords to your social media, phone, or email.
- Respecting each other's individual needs and preferences.

Although most people think that healthy relationships don't need a boost, they actually do require boosts every now and then. Often times, relationships require a boost when one or more people in the relationship are beginning to feel disconnected from their partner or feel like their relationship has gotten flat. If this is the case, it is important to find a fun activity that both people enjoy, like going on a nice drive, and have a conversation about the reasons why they want to be in this relationship. After this, it is important to keep using healthy behaviors throughout the relationship.

This book will help you with your romantic relationships by covering seven crucial topics; understanding your own relationship, what makes a relationship work, learning emotional intelligence, relationship communication, improving your own communication, conflict resolution, and spicing up your sex life. These topics cover everything from understanding what type of relationship you currently have with your partner to spicing up your sex life. Relationships are a complicated subject; everybody's relationships are different depending on who it's with, what type of relationship and your own personal communication style. This book will provide you with numerous strategies that will help you identify strengths and weaknesses within your current relationship and teach you new methods to better communicate and relate to your partner. If you are ready to take a deeper look at your own relationship and how you can improve it to become a long lasting and fulfilling relationship – continue reading now!

Chapter 1: Understanding Your Own Relationship

A crucial area in learning to improve your own relationship is to understand your own existing relationship. It is impossible to know what to improve in your relationship if you don't know your own relationship's weaknesses and areas of improvement. Different types of relationships require different strategies to improve, so identifying what your relationship type is is crucial in improving it all together. In this chapter, we will be covering the following topics; understanding emotions in a relationship, accepting yourself and your partner and attachment style interactions. By learning these following topics, you will better be able to understand where your relationship falls and cater to the strategies provided in this book to help you improve your relationship.

Understanding Emotions In Relationships

We all know that it's important to take in and understand your partner's emotions. However, we often forget that we must take our own emotions into consideration as well. Most of us are so used to paying attention to other people's feelings that we don't know how to listen to our own emotions. In this subchapter, I will walk you through how to can begin listening to your own emotions in order to better understand what you need in a relationship. When you build an understanding of what your needs are in a relationship, you can better understand what your relationship needs in general.

Listening to Your Own Feelings

Knowing how to listen to your feelings is important in having a healthy relationship. For many people, this is a challenge. We live in a world where looking inward and getting in touch with the deeper parts of yourself is not as valued as distracting yourself is. This is due in large part to the media and consumerism, where we are constantly bombarded with information, so tuning out of all of this feels nice. Also, we are being sold means of distraction everywhere we go. Looking inward and getting in touch with your feelings will take practice but once you get used to it, it will become easier. There are different ways to do this, and I will outline one of them here for you.

1. Commit To Doing So

The first step to listening to your feelings is committing to doing so. If you are not committed, it will prove difficult for you to really examine yourself without a barrier there. Once you begin listening to your feelings, you will be able to take action toward improving the things that are making you feel negative emotions, and the first step to doing this is noticing what those emotions are.

2. Notice Sensations In Your Body

Once you have committed to looking deep within yourself, you are ready to begin doing so. The best place to start is to notice when something within you feels different. When we feel emotions, we often feel them manifested somewhere in our bodies. By noticing tightness in your chest or a sinking feeling in your stomach, this usually an indication that you are experiencing some type of emotion. Even if you are not sure what the emotion is, noticing the signs within your body that signal when you are feeling an emotion, is a great first step. For many people, they will feel an emotion and act on it in an aggressive way through physical aggression or through angry words and will never look inward to really explore the feeling or what brought it up for them. Take a second now to notice how your body feels on the inside and notice any locations of tightness or feelings of unrest within your body. You may be feeling some emotions right now. Bring into your awareness the changes that happen within your body when you experience an emotion so that the next time you feel it, you notice it instead of pushing it away.

3. Give The Feelings A Name

The next step to listening to your feelings after noticing that you are feeling something is giving that feeling a name. We are all aware of emotions like fear, anger, happiness, surprise and sadness. These emotions are a good place to begin.

4. Go Deeper

As we become adults, our emotions become more complex than just the five listed above. We are able to experience deeper and more complicated emotions such as shame, anxiety, desperation, shock, doubt, ambiguity, and so on. Once you are comfortable noticing and naming your emotions in a simple way, try to look at them a little deeper and figure out if the emotion you thought was sadness is actually more disappointment for example. If you are unsure of what some of these more complex emotions may be, you can name the emotion in the simpler sense (sadness, for example) and then take this word to a thesaurus or an emotion chart online in order to see what other emotions this could be related to that could better describe exactly what you are feeling.

Giving yourself a broader vocabulary of emotions will help you to express yourself in more depth so that you can develop a deeper understanding of yourself and others can develop a deeper understanding of you as well. Naming the emotions that you feel when you notice them will allow you to express these emotions to other people in the form of nonviolent communication when the time comes.

Listening for Feelings of Your Partner

Once you are comfortable noticing your own feelings, giving them names and then getting deeper into your exploration of them, you will be able to more easily observe and understand the feelings of others. If you are unable to understand your own feelings, it will prove quite difficult to understand the feelings of your partner, even if they put them into words for you. Once you have some understanding of the feelings that you experience, you will be able to relate to someone when they tell you that they are feeling anxious for example, as you may have felt this emotion or something similar as you explored your own emotions.

The other benefit to understanding your own emotions on a deeper level is that if your partner tells you that they are feeling sad, you may be able to take this deeper in your own understanding of emotions by combining this information with the knowledge you have of nonverbal communication (such as body language or facial expressions) to determine that they may be feeling something more complex. You can observe their body language, facial expressions, and the things they have been saying to you in your conversation, combined with them telling you that they are feeling sad to determine that they may be feeling dejected or depressed. By understanding ourselves, we gain a deeper understanding of humans in general and other people we interact with.

Accepting Yourself and Your Partner

On top of understanding your own emotions and your partner's emotions, a huge part of having a healthy relationship is being able to accept yourself for who you are and your partner for who they are. Learning self-acceptance is a part of improving your self-esteem. Those with low self-esteem often struggle with practicing self-acceptance and often end up in unhealthy relationships. Let's learn a little bit more about how you can use self-acceptance to better improve your self-esteem so you can function in your relationship in a healthier way.

Self-Acceptance can be defined in three different ways:

1) Self-acceptance is the feeling of being satisfied with yourself despite your past choices or behaviors
2) Self-acceptance is being aware of your strengths and weaknesses
3) Self-acceptance is having a realistic assessment of your capabilities, talents and overall worth

In summary of those three definitions, self-acceptance is the happiness and satisfaction that you have with yourself that is needed to achieve good self-esteem. Having self-acceptance means that you are able to understand who you are, be realistic about it, and be aware of what strengths and weaknesses you have. Those who have high levels of self-acceptance tend to also have a more positive attitude, do not wish to be different from who they are, accept all traits of themselves, and are not confused with their identity.

Self-esteem is defined as having confidence in your own ability, and self-worth and self-acceptance are being aware and satisfied with all your strengths and weaknesses. Self-acceptance does not need to rely on achievement to make one feel worthy. It makes people feel worthy by simply being comfortable and happy with who they are. When one is comfortable with the person that they are, they are able to better handle conflicts and face adversity when in a relationship. Those with low self-esteem often sacrifice their own needs and happiness in order to cater to their partner which then causes relationship toxicity and codependency.

So how does self-acceptance work in the real world? Based on scientific studies, self-acceptance has 5 different stages. The first stage is Aversion. People's natural response to uncomfortable feelings or situation is either avoidance or resistance. For instance, if somebody dislikes a trait that they have, it is natural that they avoid it rather than dealing with it head-on. The second stage is curiosity. When aversion no longer works, people will become curious to learn more about their problems. This curiosity is the driving factor behind people looking to learn more about their problems. The more curious a person is, the more likely they are to having a fulfilling life. People who lack this curiosity tend to shy away from problems leading to get stuck in stage one, which is aversion. The third stage is tolerance. Those in this stage will wish that their problems will go away while enduring it the entire time. Many people in this stage still suffer the effects of their problems but are forcing themselves to tolerate it so they can go on with their everyday life. The fourth stage is allowing. As people's resistance slowly drains away, they then allow themselves to feel. Rather than just recognizing and tolerating, they acknowledge them and feel the emotions that occur. This is the stage of acceptance where they accept their problem and allows themselves to feel all the emotions that come with it. The fifth and last stage is friendship. During this, people begin to see the value that their feelings bring and decide to accept them rather than willing them to leave. They become comfortable enough to be friends with those feelings regardless if it's good or bad.

Attachment Style Interactions

Figuring out what you and your partner's attachment styles are, is important to learning more about each other. It will help you understand why your partner acts the way they do and does the things they do. There are four different types of attachment styles and we will be learning about all of them in this subchapter.

Secure Attachment Style

People with secure attachment styles showcase these following traits:

- Resilient in the face of adversity. They are capable of moving on, learning, and grieving.
- Stronger ability to handle relationship difficulties. They can discuss issues, and problem solve rather than attacking the other person.
- Tendency to have a positive view of personal interactions and relationships.
- Feel secure, both being alone and being with another person.
- Capable of drawing appropriate and reasonable boundaries when needed.
- Capable of receiving and expressing intimacy.

- Higher emotional intelligence, capable of understanding others' emotions and conveying their own.

Anxious-Preoccupied Attachment Style

People with anxious-preoccupied attachment style tend to showcase these following traits:

- Have a history of emotionally charged and turbulent relationships
- Don't like to be by themselves
- Drama oriented
- Requires constant validation and love to feel secure, negative reactions when not positively reinforced enough
- Tendency to have automatic negative thinking when interpreting the intentions of others
- Likely to have many stressors within relationships
- Likely to feel more insecure and nervous regarding their relationships

Dismissive Avoidant Attachment Style

Those with dismissive-avoidant attachment style tend to showcase these following traits:

- Likely to be passive aggressive and/or narcissistic

- Tendency to have lots of acquaintances but few close relationships
- Have commitment issues
- Prioritizes lots of other things above having a romantic relationship
- Desires emotional and physical freedom
- Avoids true intimacy
- Self-sufficient and self-directed, very independent emotionally and behaviorally

Fearful-Avoidant Attachment Style

Those with fearful-avoidant attachment style tend to showcase these following traits:

- Pushes people away and have few close relationships
- Constantly suspicious of others' actions, words, and intentions
- Fearful of intimate, physical or emotional situations
- Struggle with their own confidence and relies on others
- Desires intimacy whilst simultaneously resisting it
- Often associated with challenging life experiences like abuse, abandonment, and grief

Different Types of Romantic Relationships

Romantic relationships are one of the most complicated types of relationships. This type of relationship in western culture holds more value than other types of relationships and is most popularly portrayed in media. Traditional romantic relationships are normally between a man and a woman. Although this structure is very outdated now, romantic relationships are modernly described as when two people consensually agree to be exclusively in a relationship together where passionate love is shared. In our modern day, these types of relationships can exist between a man and a woman, a man and a man, a woman and a woman and other varieties of the gender structure. On top of that, there are also different types of romantic relationships. Love isn't something that is one-size-fits-all. It means something different to every single person but it also feels and looks different to everyone. This is why there are so many different types of romantic relationships. This is so that every single person can find the best fit for their own personality, lifestyle and concept of love. In this chapter, we will be learning about seven different kinds of romantic relationships:

1. **Monogamous Relationships:** Monogamous relationships are the relationships that people first learn about and likely think of. They are the most traditional out of all types of relationships and most often easiest for children to understand as they usually see this exhibited by their parents. The people who are in monogamous relationships only have one romantic partner or sexual partner at one time. Most people who enter monogamous relationships have the intention of remaining monogamous, although it may not stay that way.

2. **Polyamorous Relationships:** Some people choose to enter a relationship that is polyamorous instead. When a person identifies as polyamorous, it means that they are comfortable and have the desire to have more than one romantic relationship at the same time. Usually, within polyamorous couples, one or both persons will have a primary partner, a secondary partner and so forth. They have an understanding that these 'rankings' are subject to change when their personal needs change. Some people in these relationships may treat every relationship that they have as perfectly equal. Just like the theme of this book, the key to any successful relationship, especially polyamorous ones, is effective and honest communication between everybody.

3. **Open Relationships:** Open relationships are, in some ways, a blend between monogamous and polyamorous relationships. An open relationship allows both partners to have sexual relations with other people but they reserve their emotional intimacy for each other only. Each person can have as many sexual partners as they want but they will only have one romantic partner.

4. **Long-Distance Relationships:** This type of relationship is pretty self-explanatory. A long-distance relationship occurs when both people have a large distance separating their physical presence. Since these relationships lack physical intimacy due to living far apart, some people in these relationships opt for an open relationship while both people are in different places. Although the 'long-distance' aspect of this relationship is usually temporary, some couples choose and are capable of having a happy relationship while living apart indefinitely.

5. **Casual Sex Relationships:** When two people are in a casual sex relationship, they agree to have regular sex with each other and that's pretty much in. Those that are in these types of relationships can be both physically and emotionally intimate with other people as well as long as both parties are comfortable with it. Casual sex relationships can also be 'exclusive,' which means that

both people are not allowed to sleep with others. This is similar to a monogamous relationship minus the emotional connection.

6. **'Friends With Benefits' Relationships:** This type of relationship is also very similar to the casual sex relationship but with one important differentiator – a platonic and established friendship. Often times, 'friends with benefits' relationships begin when two people with an established friendship have sex out of a mutual sexual attraction. Both people behave platonically outside of the sexual relationship. Usually, this type of relationship comes to an end when one person or both persons begin to date other people.

7. **Asexual Relationships:** Some people identify as asexual which means that they don't experience sexual attraction or desire to other people. However, they still want to have a romantic relationship built on emotional intimacy. Although asexual people often choose to date other asexual people to create a relationship that is purely asexual, this is not always the case. When a person that is asexual begins a relationship with a person that is sexual, it can take place in a few different forms. The couple can decide to be entirely sexless or the asexual partner can 'compromise' by engaging in sexual activity under certain agreed circumstances. The partners can also experiment in

'pseudo sexual behavior' like cuddling or an arrangement that works for both parties.

Children, Parenting, and Extended Family

Relationships get more complicated as more and more people begin involved. Many married couples often face challenges with their children and extended family. There will be problems and conflicts that arise that are unavoidable. Learning to properly deal with it without it negatively affecting you and your partner's relationship is the key to sustaining a healthy relationship.

The trick to managing so many different people is always to utilize open communication. It is always better to over-communicate than to under-communicate. Be sure that everyone is looped into all events that are relevant to them at all times so that nobody feels left out or create an opportunity for misunderstandings to arise. When you are able to communicate with everyone regarding what is going on, you allow people to understand your perspective to avoid having any misunderstandings happen. This is the most crucial part of maintaining healthy relationships when so many other people are involved.

Chapter 2: What Makes a Relationship Work?

In this chapter, we will be taking a look at all the aspects that make a romantic relationship work. There are so many different areas in a relationship and everything needs to be balanced in order for a relationship to function in a healthy way. In this chapter, we will be discussing the following topics; identifying your strengths and problem areas, learning to find your way back to each other, building mindful relationship habits, nurturing your own fondness and admiration, brainstorming new activities together and creating shared rituals. Let's dive right in!

Identifying Your Strengths and Problem Areas

Identifying your own individual strengths and problem areas is crucial in having a healthy relationship with your partner. Everybody has their strengths and weaknesses, and being able to understand your own is important so you know which areas you can lean on and which areas you need to improve. The trick to identifying this is simply by analyzing things that people have told you in the past and asking people that are close to you what your strengths and weaknesses are. If you are analyzing your past, you will be able to analyze what types of feedback you get most often from others. This could be that you have trouble actively listening in conversations or you have the tendency to dominate conversations – ask other people to give you an honest answer about what your strengths and weaknesses are so you can begin to improve on them.

Finding Your Way Back to Each Other

All relationships have their ups and downs. Sometimes couples fall apart, and they come back together after some time apart. This is normal and for some, it is a part of the process. If you are ever having doubts about your relationship and so is your partner, take some time apart to think about yourself and your partner. Time apart helps you see what you miss about your partner and if they miss the same things too, you will certainly find your way back to one another.

Build Mindful Relationship Habits

Regardless of how long you have been in a relationship with someone, you must build healthy habits that can positively impact your relationship. This can be building better listening habits, speaking habits or thought process habits. If you know you have a bad habit of thinking negative thoughts about yourself whenever you and your partner face a problem, consider overcoming that bad habit and building a healthier one. Bad habits can get in the way in romantic relationships as it builds a barrier between you and your partner. Ask your partner if there are any bad habits that you have that negatively impact the relationship. Listen to what they have to say and take their thoughts into consideration. This will help you learn which habits to keep and which habits to get rid of in order to have more mindful relationship habits.

Nurture Your Own Fondness and Admiration

Before being able to love another person, you must learn to love yourself. Only then will you be able to respect what you need and be able to ask for it from another person. If you don't know what you need or don't respect your own needs, you are at risk of falling into a toxic relationship that causes you to neglect your own needs while fulfilling the other person's. Practice self-love and allow yourself to be fond of yourself. Admire who you are and everything you've done to get to this point in your life. Expect your partner to do the same. You must not accept anything less than respect, fondness and admiration from somebody who claims that they love you. By loving yourself every day, you are showing your partner the gold standard of how to love you.

Brainstorming New Activities Together

A common problem that people face within their relationships is boredom. If you've been with someone for numerous years, you likely have done and accomplished many things together. One fundamental aspect of a healthy relationship is being able to keep things new and fresh. You can do this by brainstorming new activities together and creating new shared rituals and traditions. This can be as simple as finding an activity that neither of you has done before and going to do it. Or, it can be as complicated as starting a new tradition over a certain holiday and sticking with it year after year. Whatever it may be, coming up with new things to do frequently will keep the relationship exciting and fulfilling. Nobody likes to do the same things day in and day out. Get creative. Think outside the box. Invite your partner to do the same and I promise you will find yourself having many new things to talk about and making memories that will last a lifetime.

Chapter 3: Learn Emotional Intelligence

When it comes to communication throughout all different types of relationships, emotional intelligence is something that everybody needs to know and learn. Emotional intelligence is especially important when it comes to professional relationships and romantic relationships. This is a trait that is highly sought after by employers and potential romantic partners all over the world. To give you a little bit of background, emotional intelligence is a term that was developed by two researchers, Peter Salavoy and John Mayer, in the field of psychology. Presently, emotional intelligence is defined as a person's ability to understand, recognize, and control their emotions. It can also be defined as a person's ability to understand, recognize, and influence the emotions of other people. In it's simplest form, EI is the ability to be aware of the fact that people's emotions drive human behaviors and have the power to impact others. When people learn how to manage their emotions, they will be able to impact themselves, their relationships, and other people positively.

What Is Emotional Intelligence?

Emotional intelligence is made up of these following components:

- **Self-awareness:** Self-awareness allows people to understand their own strengths and weaknesses. This gives them a better understanding of how to react properly to other people and in certain situations.
- **Self-regulation:** When a person has self-awareness, high EI comes into play by allowing the person to properly regulate their emotions to keep it in check when needed.
- **Motivation:** People that have high emotional intelligence tend to have more motivation, which makes them more optimistic. This causes them to have more resilience towards negativity.
- **Empathy:** People who are more successful, connecting with others usually exhibit strong traits of empathy and compassion.
- **Social skills:** A person that has high emotional intelligence likely has the social skills needed in order to showcase their respect and care for others. This is why those who have higher EI tend to get along better with people in general.

Despite the critique of this topic, emotional intelligence is a concept that has a lot of appeal to the general public. There is a lot of appeal for this topic in specific industries. Recently, a lot of employers and companies have actually incorporated personality assessments as a part of the job application process in order to identify the people who have high emotional intelligence as this is an indication to them that this person would make a better team member and leader. Those with higher emotional intelligence also make for better romantic partners, friends, and family members.

The Importance of Emotional Intelligence

The importance of emotional intelligence has significantly grown over the last few years, especially when it comes to the workplace where professional relationships are involved. Just because somebody walks into their workplace, it does not mean that all the emotions that they have felt during their day get automatically locked away. It may appear that way in most people but in reality, emotions are very existent in the workplace but they are normally controlled in order to remain professional. People often pretend that they do not have emotions while at work in order to avoid appearing unprofessional.

Emotional intelligence is very important in our society today due to how different our workplace culture is. Nowadays, professional relationships are very important because most of our work is done as a team and not as individuals. This goes the same for romantic relationships since many are fostered in the workplace due to our increasingly busy lives. More forward-thinking employers now realize that acknowledging emotions during work hours tend to foster better working environments. By fostering better working environments, this would mean that people have to be more conscious of their own feelings along with other people's feelings. Those who have higher emotional intelligence are able to be more adaptable to change, which is a skill required in our present day fast paced environment.

Although emotional intelligence is a skill and trait that brings a lot of value in all types of relationships, professional relationships are the ones that hold the greatest value for it. Throughout this chapter, we will be talking about how emotional intelligence influences romantic relationships and professional relationships.

Leaders in the workplace that have higher emotional intelligence tend to foster a team of happier employees. Potential romantic interests that have higher emotional intelligence tend to find themselves attracting more people than those with low emotional intelligence. People who have higher emotional intelligence tend to live a happier life overall due to fostering healthier relationships with everybody around them.

Here are a few methods that can help a person improve their own emotional intelligence:

- **Reflect on your emotions:** When a person does the act of reflecting on their own emotions, that is when they begin to gain self-awareness. In order for a person's emotional intelligence to grow, start by simply recognizing your own feelings and paying attention to how you act during negative situations. When you become aware of which emotions you are working with, you can begin to control and manage them properly.

- **Ask for another perspective:** Everyone's perception of reality is very different. In order to understand other people's emotions, start by asking people for their opinion of the same situation. You can ask people about their perception of what you are like during emotionally charged situations so you can get a better understanding of yourself.

- **Observe:** Once you have gained more self-awareness, start trying to get a better understanding of your own behavior. Pay attention to your emotions, and begin to observe them more closely.

- **Pause for a moment:** Stop for a moment to think about the emotions you are feeling and process them before acting on them. This may be difficult during heated situations, but with practice, it will become a habit.

- **Build more empathy:** Try to improve your empathy by understanding the 'why' behind a person's emotions or feelings. Try to step into their shoes and imagine how things would feel from their perspective.

- **Learn from criticism:** Criticism is something that nobody likes, but it is an inevitable part of life and growth. Deciding to learn from criticism rather than becoming defensive right away helps improve a person's emotional intelligence.

- **Practice:** Emotional intelligence is not something that can be improved overnight. However, by practicing the above techniques, it has been proven to be improvable through frequent practice.

Examples of High Emotional Intelligence

Since people's personalities are very different from one another, how a specific person develops their emotional intelligence will vary based on the individual. Below are a few common examples of what people with high emotional intelligence tend to behave:

- They are able to express themselves in a respectful manner and an open manner without fearing that they will offend other people
- They often show resilience when faced with adversity
- They are always flexible
- There is freedom to be creative, and that is celebrated
- They often listen actively during conversations and contribute when they have something to say
- They always listen to other people's problems and show compassion to them

When it comes to high emotional intelligence, one of the components that it helps a lot with is a person's leadership abilities. Leaders that have good EI in the workplace are able to build a team of people that are deeply connected and involved in a single vision. Romantic partners that have good EI are able to attract potential partners and build strong rapport and connections right off the bat. People with high EI are exceptionally good at navigating through complex and difficult decisions while showing great emotional response.

Don't get confused here; high emotional intelligence does not mean that someone is always positive or in a happy mood. It simply means that this person has a stronger ability to make good decisions regarding their own actions when they are faced with a difficult situation. They have the ability to process their own emotions properly in order to make decisions that aren't fueled purely by feelings.

Examples of Low Emotional Intelligence

Just like how high emotional intelligence is very sought after in professional environments and relationships, low emotional intelligence plays a significant role in the way we interact with other people in the world. People who struggle with their emotional intelligence, such as your family members, friends, employers, and coworkers, may make certain social situations tense and difficult. However, in most cases, it could be your own emotional intelligence that needs some work.

In order to give you a better understanding of what low emotional intelligence looks like, here are a few examples and indications of low emotional intelligence:

- **Getting into frequent arguments:** Everyone knows at least one person in their life that seems to be getting into constant arguments with others. Other people in your life, such as your friends, family, or sometimes even strangers, may end up in an argument with these types of people. The reason behind this is that when individuals have low EI, they struggle with understanding what other people's emotions are and will engage in arguments without being considerate about what the other person is feeling.

- **Inability to understand the feelings of others:** People who have low EI tend to be very oblivious when it comes to other people's feelings and emotions. For example, they struggle with understanding why their friends might be upset with them or why their co-workers are annoyed with them. Moreover, they often feel as if they are the ones that should be annoyed at the other people because of how other people hold expectations of them to understand their feelings. While this is very true for those people who have high emotional intelligence, people with low EI lack the ability to properly assess the feelings of other people. The mere topic of emotions tends to cause frustration and exasperation in people with low EI.

- **Thinking that everyone else is too sensitive:** People that have low EI tend to tell jokes at inappropriate moments. For instance, they may make a joke right after a funeral or a tragic event. When people don't react the way they want to their mistime jokes, the person with low EI may blame them for being too sensitive. They struggle to understand what other people are feeling and therefore struggle with understanding the emotional tone during certain situations.

- **Refusing to listen to other people's perspectives:** People that have low EI tend to feel that they are always right and will intensely defend their stance and refuse to hear what other people may have to say. These people tend to be pessimists and are very critical of other people's feelings.

- **Blaming others when things go wrong:** People who have low emotional intelligence usually don't have a good understanding of their own feelings and how that relates to them having more social problems. When things aren't going how they want it to, their first reaction is to blame the people around them. They often will blame the essence of a situation or other people's behaviors. A common rebuttal that people with low EI use is that they had 'no other choice' for what they did, and that other people are the ones being not understanding about their circumstance. They tend to feel victimized in order to avoid responsibility.

- **Inability to handle emotionally fueled situations:** When a situation arises where strong emotions begin to show, people that have low EI have trouble comprehending those feelings. They may try to flee from these situations in order to avoid having to deal with confrontation. It is also very common for these people to hide their feelings and emotions from other people.

- **Sudden emotional explosions:** Just like we learned during the chapter regarding examples of people with high EI, one of the main traits of those people is their ability to maintain and regulate their emotions. People who struggle with low EI have difficulty understanding what emotions they are experiencing and how to regulate them. They often have emotional outbursts that are unexpected and appear to be uncontrollable.

- **Maintaining friendships is difficult:** People who have low EI tend to have an insensitive and abrasive demeanor which creates difficulty when they are trying to create friendships or trying to bond with others. Since friendship is something that requires give and take from both parties, people with low EI struggle with having and maintaining friendships where the sharing of emotional support, emotions, and compassion are required.

- **Lack of empathy:** Due to the fact that some people that have low EI struggle with understanding what other people's emotions are, they often struggle with feeling empathy for others. They simply do not understand what emotions other people may be feeling, so it makes it difficult for them to see things from another perspective, let alone empathize.

Chapter 4: Communication in Relationships

Relationships rely on communications to succeed. If just one person has bad communication skills, it can negatively affect the relationship drastically. This is why understanding what basic communication is will be extremely helpful in improving and growing your relationship. Although people communicate with one another on a daily basis, most of us don't think about how we do it and what communication actually entails. We all have our own unique habits and we likely communicate similarly on a day to day basis. In this chapter, we are going to change that up a little bit. We will learn the basics of communication, learn about how communication skills affect your romantic relationships and learn about some guidelines for couple disputes. If you have any predispositions about your own communication skills or your partner's, scrap that now and begin re-learning.

Communication Ground Rules

The ground rules of communication are fairly simple and can be described in two words; open communication. Depending on who the person is that you're in a relationship with, they may have higher or lower EI skills. Being able to communicate openly is the best way to avoid any assumptions and misunderstandings. In order to understand the importance of ensuring open communication in your romantic relationships, I will teach you about how communication skills can affect your romantic relationships.

How Communication Skills Affect Your Romantic Relationships

Communication skills play a crucial role in your romantic relationships. Without proper communication skills, you might as well flush your relationship down the toilet. In this subchapter, we are going to look at how having good (or bad) communication skills can impact your relationships.

If you are a good communicator, this means you are able to;

1. Listen effectively and actively
2. Observe your own thoughts and feelings
3. Know when a response is not needed
4. Observe other people and practice empathy
5. Form thoughtful and appropriate responses according to your observations of yourself and others, through empathy

By being able to do all of these things, you are able to connect with people on a deeper level through understanding. You are able to share information with people effectively and receive information as well. These five points are beneficial in all types of relationships. Relationships are all about connection, and connection is difficult without the ability to be a good communicator.

How Bad Communication Affects Relationships

If you are a person who struggles with good communication, you may find it difficult to interact with people in professional and personal settings. If you are not able to listen to the people around you and are unable to express yourself through verbal communication, then reaching mutual understanding in your relationships will prove quite difficult. Being able to observe your own thoughts and feelings and explain these to other people through writing or speaking, for example, is very important and being unable to or ineffective at this can lead to miscommunications or misunderstandings in your relationships.

Bad communication is not always in the form of mean words being exchanged or voices being raised. In most cases, bad communication is a lack of communication. When certain things are not acknowledged or said, both people begin to assume things about one another and conclusions will be drawn. In order to avoid having bad communication in relationships, over-communication should be used in said. By over-communicating your intentions and your thoughts, the receiving person begins to get an understanding of your style of communication and thought processes. The more they learn about what goes on in your head, the less they will misinterpret you. This is especially important at the beginning of relationships as that's where the biggest learning curve is. This holds true not only for romantic relationships, but for professional, personal, and familial relationships as well. Just like how you probably have a strong understanding of the way your best friend thinks and communicates, you should know that you have a weak understanding of the way your new coworker thinks and feels and vice versa. In order to avoid any misunderstandings and arguments, be sure to over-communicate to leave no room for misinterpretations. Once you and the other person have developed an understanding, the two of you can form your own style of communication that works for both parties.

Fighting in Relationships Is a Form of Communication

Fighting now and then is inevitable, but the way that you fight is the important part. Fighting is a type of communication that involves both verbal and nonverbal communication. If you are the type of person that screams and yells when you are fighting, you are likely not listening to the other person in an active way and this may be something that causes problems for you in your relationship. Being able to fight healthily is an important part of communication in relationships. There are many different ways to fight, and you can employ empathy to observe and understand the way your partner fights in order to respond accordingly. Some people turn quiet and will not speak when they are fighting. While this is not an effective form of communication, being able to recognize this in another person will help you to become a better communicator. By understanding the way that your partner fights, you are able to respond in a way that will lead to a resolution and a strengthening of the relationship. If your partner becomes quiet and will not engage in dialogue during a fight, you can use empathy to understand that they may be feeling angry and hurt and may need some time to process their emotions before sharing them. You can say something like "why don't we take thirty minutes apart, and then revisit this after." By doing this, you are showing your partner that you understand what they need and that you are willing to give this to them. You are not lying down and admitting defeat; you are simply using your knowledge of communication to choose the most effective way to communicate in your relationship. This is a sign of mature and effective communication. By giving your partner this time to themselves, they may come back after those thirty minutes willing to discuss calmly with you and communicate effectively. By approaching arguments in this way, you will be able to examine the situation as is progresses, respond accordingly and therefore choose the most effective type of communication.

Basic Communication Skills

Everybody has the ability to use basic communication, this ability is something that we are born with, but this does not mean that everybody can communicate with skill. This basic communication includes things like being able to speak, being able to recognize and tell someone what your basic needs are, like being hungry, or having to go to the bathroom. Basic communication also includes being able to hear what another person is saying to you and understanding what it means. We take these types of communication for granted as we use them so commonly, but they are a part of communication. This can be taken much further however, as there are many small and subtle things that people communicate without saying a word. This type of communication is called nonverbal communication. The other two types which we learn quite early on in life and must be taught in order to know, are written and visual communication. In this section, we will look at all of these a little closer to give you an idea of which ones you may be good at and those that you may be lacking insight into.

Four Types Of Communication

As I mentioned earlier, there are four main types of communication. All of these types are equally as important and will require different techniques to master. We will be exploring verbal, nonverbal, written, and visual communication. Depending on the relationship type you have with the person you're communicating with and the situation you are in, you may be using one or more of these types. For instance, if you are communicating with your significant other over the phone, the only type of communication you will be using is verbal. In that scenario, you would want to practice good verbal communication techniques. However, if you are in the workplace communicating with your manager, you may be using both verbal, written, visual, and non-verbal communication depending on if you are communicating with your manager physically or not. This book will help you learn each of these types and how to best communicate. Let's take a look at them:

Verbal

The first type of communication that we will examine is that which is likely the first to come to mind when you hear the word "communication." Verbal communication is the type that is used between people that uses words and sounds. This is the type of communication we use when we are meeting someone for the first time or learning more about a person over coffee. This type of communication involves the language and dynamics of speech. Verbal communication is innate to humans, as we are all built to learn and use language to communicate with other humans.

This form of communication can become quite complicated when looked at in-depth. Think about sarcasm, for example, and how when using sarcasm, you are saying one thing but meaning the exact opposite. For example, "this is fun" when said in a sarcastic tone actually means "this is no fun at all." It takes skill in communication to use and understand this type of verbal communication. The most important components of verbal communication are the actual words that are spoken and the tone of voice that it's said in. Tone of voice is more important than the actual words said. Just like the sarcasm example, you could be saying, "Wow, this is great!" but mean the complete opposite. In order to master verbal communication, you must understand how different tones carry entirely different meanings.

Nonverbal

Even if you speak a different language than someone else, you are still able to communicate with them. This is because of another type of communication called nonverbal communication. Nonverbal communication is a term that includes a wide variety of ways that people communicate things that they are thinking or feeling without using words. This becomes a type of communication when thoughts and feelings are communicated in the things that people do (or do not do) such as body language, eye movements, eye contact or facial expressions.

Humans are quite selective about what they choose to share with others, but sometimes the things that they would rather hide become apparent through their displays of nonverbal communication. This type of physical, bodily communication can be either a conscious or unconscious action, meaning that we may not even know that we are sharing our thoughts, feelings or opinions in ways other than through our words. It is important to understand this type of communication because you may be able to pick up on things that people are displaying to you without them even saying a word to you. It is also important because having good communication skills will also help you to be aware of what you may be sharing with others through your body language.

Since body language makes up 50% of a person's entire communication, focusing on the way you are carrying yourself and your facial expressions will help you deliver your message effectively. By carrying yourself effectively and understanding what your body language is portraying, you will be able to deliver your messages properly so that the appropriate meaning is expressed.

Visual

Visual communication can be seen similarly to nonverbal communication, but in this case, we are going to look at it in terms of things like art and graphs. Visual communication is anything that conveys information to you through your eyes that is not involving a person and their body. This can be a photograph, a letter, a chart, or a drawing. This type of communication can be used in addition to other forms but can also be seen on its own. As you may have heard in the past, different people have different learning styles. What this means is that some people digest information better through hearing and speaking, some through feeling and doing and some through seeing. This last type of learning style involves visual forms of communication as the best form for this type of person to understand the information that is being communicated.

Sometimes in a relationship such as a teacher and student or a workplace relationship, one person may prefer to have a picture drawn for them if they are better able to understand by seeing a concept depicted for them in a graph or a drawing. In this case, the person trying to communicate with them may want to use this method instead, in order to get their point across in the best way possible. Being aware of the different types of communication and the ways in which they can be used is helpful when trying to think of creative ways to explain concepts or ideas.

There is no right way to communicate as there are many, many different ways to do so.

Written

The final form of communication that we will look at is written communication. Written communication involves the use of words or symbols to communicate an idea of a message or a concept. This is used every day in signage for example. This is also used very commonly at this point in time as email and instant message communication is a very popular type of communication. This is another type of communication that cannot be done if you do not know the same language or alphabet as another person and is one that requires the same language skills first.

Sometimes in a romantic relationship, a person will feel more comfortable writing a letter than speaking about their feelings verbally. This can prove beneficial to the relationship as the person can still get their feelings out, and they can be understood by their partner, but they are not forced to try to think of the best way to say them aloud on the spot. In a more professional or a friend relationship, this can also prove useful. Some people are better able to communicate their thoughts when they can write them out rather than speaking them aloud.

Written communication is heavily used in a place of work. The way a person writes their emails, reports, and any other type of message makes a huge difference in how the receiving person perceives it. In a professional workplace, it is always better to follow proper business etiquette when writing emails and communications. You also want to make sure that the tone you are writing in will be well-received by the other person. For instance, if you are emailing a customer, you want to make sure your emails are friendly but also professional. The way you email a customer should not be the same as the way you would email your best friend or your mother.

Communication Guidelines for Ideological Disputes

Almost every single couple in the world has experienced their own unique ideological disputes. This is unavoidable as no two people will be exactly the same. The key to moving past disputes that arise from different ideological stances is simply to listen to the other person and try to understand where they are coming from. Although the two of you may never agree on a certain topic, listening to the other person makes them feel heard and understood. Listening does not mean agreeing, but it certainly does make the other person feel valued. This goes the same for your partner as well. They don't necessarily have to agree to all your ideas; they just have to listen to them and try their best to understand.

The problem with listening to different ideas sometimes is that a person may simply just be hearing you but not listening to you. There is a big difference between hearing and listening. You may hear the individual words that a person is saying, but this is not the same as understanding the sentences they are saying and the entire concept as a whole. Further, if you are simply hearing. But not listening, you likely would forget what the person had been talking about just a few short minutes after the conversation.

When you are only hearing someone and not listening to them, it is actually a type of violent communication. When you and your partners have ideological differences, violent communication is normally the starting point for further disputes. When a person begins to used violent communication, most of the focus is on the self. The person using this type of communication is usually more concerned with their own ideas, how they are presenting themselves, and how they want to get what they want more than anything else. Due to this, they are likely only hearing the other person but not putting any effort into really listening and understanding it.

Instead, nonviolent communication should be used during discussions of each other's ideologies. Listening is very important in these discussions. Since nonviolent communicators are concerned with the well-being of the people they interact with and playing a part in improving this well-being, they place importance on listening and understanding the person in order to know how best they can contribute to the betterment of the other person.

Another place where this becomes important is when listening to your internal monologue. By this point in your life, you are so used to your internal monologue and the sound of your thought voice that you likely do not even notice it most of the time. When it comes to hearing and listening, you want to ensure you are listening to your thoughts rather than just hearing them. Doing this will help you become aware of the ways in which you talk to yourself. Are you using violent communication when you speak to yourself, ridiculing, shaming, and judging yourself? This may be something that you notice by listening to your thoughts. By becoming aware of your internal voice, you will be able to begin also using nonviolent communication with yourself, as it is just as important, if not more important, to be able to speak to yourself in a gentle and understanding way.

When you are able to listen to yourself and your partner in a nonviolent manner, you can slowly begin to understand their views regardless of how different they are. The definition of the word *understanding* includes words sympathetically, aware, forgiving, tolerant and feelings. This means that listening and understanding go hand in hand. The best way to develop an understanding is by listening, asking thoughtful questions and concentrating.

Chapter 5: Improving Your Communication

Communication is the cornerstone of all relationships. At this point in the book, you should have learned enough to understand that most relationship problems stem from improper communication. This can be in the form of not being able to listen properly, understand correctly, and not being able to voice your thoughts properly. The simplest way to begin improving your communication skills is to practice active listening. In this chapter, we will be covering three main topics to help you better communicate with your partner; learning to utilize active listening, different types of effective communication styles and learning to engage and connect with your partner more frequently.

Develop Active Listening

Active listening is something that is becoming harder and harder as our society gets more fast-paced and distractions are continuously increasing in our everyday environments. Do you ever find yourself drifting off if someone is telling you a story from their Friday night? Or do you find it hard to concentrate if someone is talking to you about something that you don't have the interest? Well, this is because our minds are conditioned to love instant gratification. If what the other person is saying isn't bringing instant gratification to our bodies, you likely will struggle with paying attention to what they're saying. This is one of those things that is quite an easy fix. Simply try to ignite the curiosity within yourself. Get yourself curious about other things, even if you have never had an interest in that topic. Try to really listen and visualize what the other person is saying. This way, questions begin to emerge and that is when a conversation begins to happen organically. For example, if your new coworker is telling you about their love for gardening, visualize what is happening as they are telling you about what they gardened this weekend. Ask them questions about their story, and soon, a conversation is flowing and you will have the opportunity to share your interests and stories with them as well. Healthy relationships are two-sided; both people have to have the chance to share their thoughts and feelings and receive support from the other person. Practice active listening with everyone around you so that you can exercise it on your partner.

Active listening is something that can help make you an effective listener and, therefore, an effective communicator. Active listening involves not just hearing what is being said to you, but taking it in and trying to understand it as well. Many times we will hear the person speaking to us, but we will not really be paying attention to what they are saying. Paying close attention helps us to really understand the information being shared with us and then to respond accordingly. This type of listening will help you to get the most out of your communications no matter who they are with.

The second thing to note when becoming a better listener is your intention. Many times we will listen with the intent to respond. Instead of paying close attention to the person we are speaking to, we are listening for the end of their turn so that we can say what we want to say. We may also be thinking of what we want to say next for the entire duration that the other person is speaking. Instead, we want to listen with the intent to understand. Listening requires an open mind. If our mind is full of thoughts about how we will respond and what we will say next, then we are unable to really listen and process what we are hearing. We may even think that we are listening, but it may not be in the most effective way for good communication.

If we can actively listen with the intent to really hear and understand rather than the intent to play our own part in the conversation, we can develop a greater understanding of other people and what they are saying to us, in order to then decide how we want to contribute to the conversation, and the best way to do so.

One key part of nonverbal communication that is often overlooked is the things that people do not say. Pay attention to what is avoided or left out. That is to say, read between the lines. If your partner only talks about something specific or is obviously avoiding certain topics altogether, this can give you information about them. In some instances, the things people do not say can tell us more about them than what they do say. If we had not been listening very closely, we might not even notice what they left out or we may not remember if they did or did not mention certain things. Listening intently allows you to be sure that they avoided certain things

Another thing that makes a good listener is the ability to communicate while listening. This does not mean that you are talking over them or nodding furiously though. This involves gently telling the person that you are hearing them. There will be appropriate moments in a conversation where you can tell the person that you understand them, that you are hearing them and that you are listening to them. This will make them feel heard and in turn, they will be more inclined to continue sharing their words with you. The second part of this is being able to ask questions. Sometimes you will want to ask questions, especially if you have been listening closely and trying to understand the person. If you need clarification or would like the person to further explain something, it is acceptable to ask for clarification of a specific point or concept. The other person will likely welcome the active listening you are doing (that involves asking questions) the commitment to understanding and the interest you are showing in what they are saying.

Active listening also encompasses non-judgment. It involves being able to not judge what a person is about to say before they even say it. It is in our human nature to judge other people. However, it doesn't mean that it is not something that can't be changed. Especially in our modern society, everything is so connected through the internet and social media, simply looking at a person's picture online can cause a series of assumptions and judgments to be made about them, even if you have never met this person.

This type of behavior tends to limit people from meeting different types of people that they could possibly hit it off with, but due to their physical appearance or your perception of them, you may have avoided getting to know them. Start by just paying attention to the thoughts that you have when you first meet someone. If you notice that your thoughts become judgmental such as "Oh, he must be insecure since all he talks about is working out." Or "She must be so weird since she only posts pictures of her cats." Or "He probably is a loser because of the clothes he's wearing." Simply just ask yourself why you are thinking about those things. Most of the times your answer will probably "I don't know!" Our minds are conditioned by society at this point to judge a person immediately just based on their physical appearance. When these thoughts occur, simply acknowledge them but don't let them affect the way you see this person.

By actively listening to your partner and not allowing yourself to make judgments about them or what they're about to say will showcase that you have the ability to listen and understand your partner. When a person feels understood by another person, they are much more likely to communicate with you in the same way back.

Developing Effective Communication

Now that you have learned about active listening and preventing judgment, you are ready to learn some more complicated communication styles. In this subchapter, I will be teaching you about 19 different types of effective communication skills that are beneficial for couples. These techniques can be used to develop deeper connections, a greater understanding between you and another person, or take your relationship to the next level.

We will begin by looking at the term "effective communication," which we have seen over and over in this book so far. What exactly is effective communication though? Effective communication is essentially all of the topics that we discussed in the previous chapter put together to make an individual who is very effective at communication. It is those five points that we saw in chapter four which I will now remind you of here;

1. Listen effectively and actively
2. Observe your own thoughts and feelings
3. Know when a response is needed and when it is not
4. Observe other people's words and actions and practice empathy
5. Form thoughtful and appropriate responses according to your observations of yourself and others, through empathy

6. Deliver your words or actions in a clear manner so that they can be easily understood

7. Speak in an articulate manner with effective choice of words

When trying to determine whether you are an effective communicator or whether you need to work on your communication skills, you can look at the frequency with which misunderstandings occur in your relationships and interactions. This is a good indication of how effectively you are able to listen and to speak, as the more effective your communication skills, the fewer misunderstandings you should have. You may be saying, "but what if I am a great communicator but the other person is not?" If this is the case, you should still be able to listen actively in order to ask for clarification where needed, thus allowing you to resolve any possible misunderstandings or miscommunications. Even if the other person needs to work on their communication skills, if you are an effective communicator, you should be able to effectively direct the interaction in order to get the information you need from the person. You should also be able to speak in a clear and articulate manner so that you are able to effectively get your points across and ensure that you are not being misunderstood.

Communication Techniques

In this section, we will look at various techniques for effective communication that can help you to improve your communication skills in your relationships and all of your interactions. These techniques include things to say or do in order to ensure you understand your partner and that they understand you effectively.

Silence

The first technique we will talk about is the "power of silence." Using silence in your communication may seem counter-intuitive, but it is highly effective. Remember how in chapter three, we talked about nonverbal communication and how it can tell us a lot about other people. This is similar; however, this type of communication is actually verbal. This type of verbal communication involves inserting silence strategically into your conversation. This can be used to get more information from your partner if you are not getting enough information from them. As we discussed in the previous section, being a good communicator involves being able to get as much information from the other person as you can to avoid misunderstandings. You can use silence to do so. If you pause and wait, this can give your partner time to collect their thoughts and share them with you. This can also show them that you are listening and giving them time to talk, without having them feel rushed or pressured. This involves being able to be silent and wait, and you must avoid rushing to speak as soon as there is silence in the conversation. Being comfortable with silence is another attribute of effective communicators.

Mirroring

Another way that you can encourage your partner to share information with you if you feel that you are not able to clearly understand their communication is to mirror them. What this means is that you will use your tone of voice, your body positioning, your choice of words, and your general demeanor to bring it to their level. For example, if your partner is sitting upright, speaking with full sentences, and inserting long, thoughtful pauses after their sentences, you can do something similar when you are speaking as well. This will help to make them feel comfortable and understood. Another example is if they are slouching in their chair, using a lot of slang and speaking very slow, you can emulate some of this as well. This will make them feel like you understand them and can help them to understand you better. If you meet them at their choice of vocabulary and tone of voice, they are more likely to understand what you are saying than if you had chosen the opposite type of communication as them.

Request Feedback

Asking for feedback while communicating is another effective technique that is used by good communicators. By asking for feedback during an interaction, it avoids miscommunications and misunderstandings. This is because if there are any parts of the conversation that are confusing to one person, they can be addressed then and there, instead of becoming a bigger misunderstanding later on. Requesting feedback can be as simple as saying something like, "what do you think?" or "how does that sound to you?" by saying one of these things, or something like it, you can confirm that the person has understood you by listening to their response. You can also say something like, "does this make sense to you?" Or "do you know what I mean?" Asking in this way is more direct and can help you ensure that the person knows you are asking them to confirm their understanding. This way, if there is a misunderstanding, you can address this later on, how you asked them to ask for clarification if they needed it. You can also take time to ask if they have any questions periodically, so that they may feel comfortable enough to clarify things with you.

Cultivate Curiosity

By being genuinely curious about your partner and what they have to say, you will automatically listen more intently, appear more enthusiastic and genuinely have an easier time remembering what they were talking about later on. In romantic relationships, this is a given, as you are curious about the person you are with and that is why you are with them. This technique is something that we can look at our romantic relationships for. When the person you love is talking to you about their day, you are genuinely curious and interested in how their day was. This makes you a good listener and communicator, as you will ask questions and give feedback. You can use this approach in your other relationships to show the person that you are interested and attentive. This technique will help you to deepen your connections and make your relationships last longer. It is possible to cultivate a genuine curiosity where it was not before, as you can become interested in someone just by trying to get to know them better.

Forget Yourself

This next technique can also be referred to as "Ego Suspension." What this means is putting yourself aside and allowing the other people in the conversation to share more about themselves. Most of the time, conversations move from one topic to the next, with each person involved sharing their own opinions of the topic and how it relates to their life. This usually results in a lot of surface-level topic discussion and not much depth about any one topic. When someone is an effective communicator; however, they are able to put themselves aside and listen to the other people or person speak about their thoughts about a topic in more detail. They are able to let go of their thoughts about the topic or the need to share their own opinions about it and listen to the other people share their thoughts. This allows the conversation to get deeper as the person speaking has the time and space to speak on a deeper level before the other person jumps in with their experience of it.

That is not to say that a conversation is not a mutual exchange of ideas, opinions, and experiences, but that being an effective communicator involves knowing when to let the other person continue speaking and when is the time to share your own side.

Positivity

Positivity may not seem like it would be included in a list of techniques for communication, but it can prove quite beneficial to connection and relationships. By being positive during an interaction, helps the other person to feel safe and comfortable which will allow them to be open and receptive to sharing themselves with you. By being negative or pessimistic during an interaction, it can cause the other person to become defensive and closed off, preventing them from sharing themselves with you.

Positivity helps your relationships because it makes the other person feel comfortable, which is an important part of developing a connection or deepening the connection that is already present.

Enthusiasm

Communicating with enthusiasm is similar to using positivity to make your partner feel comfortable communicating with you. By being enthusiastic, it makes people feel like what they are saying is of interest to you. This makes them feel happy and accepted. You can use enthusiasm by inserting some words like "yes!" into appropriate moments when your partner is speaking. Saying small words like this in an enthusiastic manner that does not come across forced will help your interactions to feel positive and productive.

Humor

Using humor takes skill, but when used at the right times, it can be a great way to lighten a serious mood or relieve the tension of a serious conversation. It can also help to ease the tension in a situation where there are a lot of nerves or one person is feeling nervous. Humor can help to communicate the fact that there is a need for seriousness sometimes, but that this does not mean there is anger or resentment present. Humor, when used correctly, can also help you to tell a person something that they may find offensive or be hurt by in a softer and lighter manner.

Open-Ended Questions

Using open-ended questions to your advantage is extremely beneficial when you are communicating with someone who is not as skilled of a communicator. Because they may be more resistant to sharing things or they may explain things in a way that is hard to understand, asking questions can help you to ensure you are properly understanding the person and avoid misunderstandings. By asking questions that are to be answered with a yes or a no however, this will not give you much more information. You must ask questions that are to be answered with a full sentence in order to get more information out of the person. An example of an open-ended question could be, "what do you hope to get out of this interaction?" This question must be answered using one or more full sentences and cannot be answered by one word like yes or no. Asking questions like this will help the person if they have a hard time communicating effectively because this will help to direct the conversation for them and tell you what you really want to know.

This can be used in professional, friendship, romantic, or any other relationships. This type of technique is what sets apart the mediocre from the effective communicators.

Expressing Approval

By giving approval to your partner when you are interacting with them, it will usually encourage them to keep talking. This can get your partner to open up as it helps them to feel accepted and not judged. This will open their mind and leave them willing to share their thoughts with you. This one must be done earnestly, as people are good at telling when other people are being ingenuine. This can come in the form of saying something like, "wow, I love this about you" or something of the like. Try to ensure that it is something true you are saying so that it comes across that way.

Eye Contact

Eye contact is a form of nonverbal communication that communicates a great deal to your partner. The amount of eye contact someone is making is an indicator of their level of comfort in the situation as well as an indicator of the intentions of a person. Giving too much eye contact will make the person feel uncomfortable and even humiliated, as this gives the impression that you are making fun of them by over-showing the fact that you are listening to them. If someone is avoiding eye contact altogether, they tend to seem very uncomfortable and maybe even untrustworthy, almost as if they are trying very hard to hide something from you. We have all encountered an uncomfortable amount of eye contact, whether too much or too little, where it made us feel like something was not right. You may have been feeling unease but were unaware as to why. Feeling someone's eyes staring directly into yours with no end in sight makes for a lot of discomfort while trying to catch someone's eye, which is clearly making an effort to avoid yours makes for a very awkward conversation. If someone is making steady eye contact, looking away every now and then and then coming back to meet your eyes once again, they are probably feeling comfortable in the situation or conversation and are quite secure with themselves. This amount of eye contact makes us feel comfortable in the other person's presence and feel that their intentions are pure.

The amount of eye contact you give therefore, will show your partner how you are feeling in their presence. You want to show them that you are comfortable and listening to them, and do not want to make the interaction awkward, so be aware of your eye contact during conversations and what messages it may be sending.

Eliminating Filler Words

You are likely aware of filler words such as *um, like,* and *so.* These tend to be inserted into our vocabulary when we are nervous or feeling unsure, or maybe even just as a short break when we are gathering our thoughts. These words can make it seem like we are very uncomfortable or unsure and this is usually not the message we want to be sending. In any sort of relationship, there come times when we may feel nervous or unsure but avoiding these words and instead choosing to pause silently or insert different more specific words will help you to be a better and more effective communicator. As we discussed in our first technique of this section, silence is a great tool sometimes and can often be a better choice than inserting the word "um" or "like."

Open Communication

Just as you know from talking to other people, when someone is very closed-off and refuses to talk about themselves, it can make you uncomfortable as you may be wondering why they are hiding from you and if there is a reason why you should be doing the same. This is important to remember, as many of the techniques we discussed so far have had to do with listening and not talking about yourself too much. There does, however, have to be a balance. Being an effective communicator is about knowing when the right times to share are, and that you have to share some things with the other person if you want them to share things with you. Not only does this help them to feel comfortable, but it will lead to a deeper relationship. A connection cannot be one-sided in terms of sharing information and receiving information. It must be a mutual exchange of yourselves with the other person. This allows you to get to know each other and form an evolving relationship.

Avoiding Information Overload

While it is important to share information clearly and articulately with your partner, it would not matter how clearly you were explaining if there was simply too much information for the person to process. When sharing information with the other person, you want to ensure you are not bombarding them with too much. You want to ensure that they are able to process what you are saying in order to form thoughtful responses. You want to ensure that you are speaking concisely and are sticking to the point, especially in your professional relationships.

This works the other way as well. If a person is telling you way too much information that you cannot process it all in time to think about what they have said and formed a thoughtful response, you can try to insert a few questions in order to clarify or slow down the relaying of information.

'Same Team' Communication

This is quite a simple technique but one that goes a long way in terms of effectively communicating. By adding words into your sentences such as "us," "our," and "we," this will show your partner that you are with them and are on the same side as them. This will encourage them to feel comfortable and that you understand them, even before they have shared anything with you. This helps you to create a bond with another person which is very important and helpful in your relationship.

Speaking As Equals

When people feel like you are their equal, it makes them more receptive to what you are saying and opens them up to listen to what you have to say. When you speak to someone as if they are below you or less than you, it can leave them feeling defensive and insecure. When someone is feeling insecure, it is hard for them to be their true self. Especially in romantic relationships and friendships, it is important for both people to feel that they are equals and that their relationship is a mutual exchange of caring and love, not a relationship where one person is there for the other person and that it is not reciprocal.

To show your partner that you see them as an equal, it is important to focus on the words that you are saying and not on how to deliver them in an authoritative way. This is similar to coming to their level with your choice of words and body language, as you will want to communicate to them in a way that they will best understand, regardless of their position in relation to you.

Saying Their Name

This technique is more useful when it comes to those professional relationships, but it is important, nonetheless. By using your partner's name periodically in conversation, it shows them that you care enough to remember and use their name and that you are being attentive to them and your interaction with them. This makes people feel comfortable and secure with you and will lead them to feel like you care for them as a person and not just another human.

Empathy

Empathy is an important component of communication that allows you to connect with the person and their feelings. Here, empathy can be useful as a communication technique in another way as well. Using empathy when talking to your partner can give you insight into what they may decide to do and what they may prefer when given a choice. This can be beneficial in a romantic relationship when trying to anticipate things, or in a professional relationship when trying to determine how someone would perform in a promotion, for example. Being able to use empathy in a variety of ways when it comes to communication will do nothing but help your communication skills to go from simple to advanced.

Connect and Engage Daily

The only way you can improve communication with your partner is to practice as frequently and as often as you can. Not only will this help you understand your partner's communication style, but it will help you practice communication techniques that work best with them. You will also be able to get to know them even better regardless of how well you think you know them now. There are always more things to learn about someone.

Make an effort to speak with your partner daily and assess their body language and communication style. The more you analyze them and communicate your own feelings, the stronger the understanding that you will develop for them. Your partner will be able to see this and will also have the opportunity to learn more about your specific communication styles and ideologies. Being able to connect and engage with your partner daily is a great way to practice communicating whilst getting to know each other better at the same time. Do not neglect this; practice with them every day whether it's in person, over the phone, or over text message.

Chapter 6: Conflict Resolution

In this chapter, I will be teaching you the importance of conflict resolution and how to do it peacefully. As we all know, every relationship will come across conflict and their own set of arguments. How you approach conflict is extremely important as it can make or break your relationship. In this chapter, we will be focusing on all topics related to conflict resolution; the importance of them, coping with solvable relationship problems, violent communication, and nonviolent communication, learning to use nonviolent communication during conflicts and restoring trust after conflict. Remember, conflicts are normal within relationships and the purpose isn't to avoid any conflict possible. The point is to accept that conflicts do happen but to learn how to navigate through it so that you and your partner can find a solution to strengthen the relationship.

Conflict Resolution Skills Are Important

Since conflict and arguments are an unavoidable part of life, it is important to learn how to communicate yourself during situations like that. While it may seem like there are a lot of things to remember, it will come more naturally the more you practice it. This subchapter will focus on providing you with techniques and examples on how to express yourself during arguments and conflicts. Making judgments, blaming, yelling, shaming, and so on are types of communication styles that you don't want to use during conflicts. As long as you remember these points, you will be able to express yourself in a nonviolent way and the steps will come back to your memory. Even if you are not following the steps too closely, as long as you are ensuring that you are not using violent communication, you will be much closer to using nonviolent communication than if you had forgotten everything you learned entirely.

Violent Communication Vs. Nonviolent Communication

In this subchapter, we will look at the difference between violent and nonviolent communication so that you have an idea of how to tell them apart. Now that you know what communication is on a basic level, we can dive a little bit deeper and learn the difference between these two methods of communication. There is a very thin line between violent and non-violent communication, in order for a person to learn how to communicate non-violently, they must be able to distinguish the two. Let's dive right in.

Violent Communication

Oftentimes while communicating, especially in times of conflict, people will use means of communication that can be considered "violent." While this does not mean physical violence, we can be violent in the way that we communicate. What this means is communicating in a way that results in harm to someone else or to ourselves. Violent communication is a means of communication that includes any number of the following;

- Judging
- Shaming
- Criticizing
- Ridiculing
- Demanding
- Coercing
- Labeling
- Threatening
- Blaming
- Accusing

When any or all of the following are present in our communications, we are using violent communication. Communicating in this way has negative impacts on the people with whom we are communicating. As this is violent communication, it causes internal harm. If we are communicating intrapersonally in this way, we may cause harm to ourselves. If we communicate in this way with others, we can cause internal harm to others. In time, this type of communication can lead to anger and resentment, and if we speak to ourselves in this way, it can eventually lead to depression.

Oftentimes, we don't even know we are using violent communication, as it may be quite a normal way of interacting for us. Many societies model violent communication and thus, the people who grow up in them don't realize that there is any other way to communicate. This causes may interactions to be full of anger and hate and involve raised voices and harsh words. Sometimes, this leads to physical violence.

Violent communication aims to lower a person's feelings of self-worth, ignores their needs, and is void of compassion. It can happen on both the part of the speaker and the listener. Below are some examples of different forms of violent communication for your reference.

1. Moral Judgement or Evaluation
"Jennifer is lazy."

In this example, the speaker is using judgment. They are also labeling Jennifer and being critical of her. They are evaluating her and doing so in a judgmental way. In this type of violent communication, the speaker often sees the other person as being wrong.

2. Denying Responsibility

"It's not my fault; the policy states that I have to fire you."

In this example of violent communication, the speaker is refusing to take responsibility for their own actions and blaming them on policies, regulations, and rules. In this type of example, the person may also blame their thoughts or feelings on other people or on rules, social rules or anything other than their own decision-making.

3. Demanding

"You need to do my homework for me."

In this type of example, the speaker is implying (or sometimes explicitly stating) that there is the threat of punishment, of having to take the blame or of losing a reward if they do not comply with the demand. This type can also be seen in the reverse, where there is the implication of a reward if the person complies with the demand. This is a manipulative form of communication which is also a type of demand.

4. Lack of Compassion

"Were you really sick yesterday, or did you just not feel like showing up?"

In this type of example, *lacking compassion,* there are numerous ways that this can show up in an interaction. At its core, this type of violent communication involves the speaker intentionally sounding like they are trying to fix a situation but doing so in a way that involves correcting the listener, shutting them down, trying to educate them, one-upping them or interrogating them. In this way, the speaker is not showing compassion but instead is trying to be the voice of reason where it was not solicited.

While the person communicating in a violent way may not realize it, it can result in the listener following along with whatever the request is out of feelings of obligation, fear of punishment, shame, fear, or guilt. Because of this, this type of communication can be quite manipulative and controlling, as it forces the actions of others.

You may get what you want out of creating this type of situation, but the ways that it can impact your relationships and your mental health negatively are worth mentioning. Firstly, if you speak to others in this way, the chances that you speak to yourself in this way as well are quite high. By not being compassionate or empathetic to others, you are likely unaware of how to be compassionate or empathetic to yourself. This means that your mental health and your emotional wellbeing will suffer. By learning how to use compassion and empathy toward others, you will learn how to use it in your intrapersonal interactions as well. Secondly, by speaking violently toward others, it can cause your relationships to suffer. If you speak to your family members, such as your children in this way in order to get them to do what you want, they will more than likely develop feelings of resentment toward you. This becomes a discussion of whether it is worth it to you to have the actions of others controlled by your words, or if you would rather have strong and genuine relationships that don't involve fear, shame and guilt.

Nonviolent Communication

Contrary to violent communication is nonviolent communication. Nonviolent Communication (NVC) is often called compassionate communication. This type of communication is the exact opposite of the type of violent communication that we just finished discussing above. NVC enables freedom of choice, involves the understanding of feelings, values and needs, focuses on equality and most of all, prioritizes compassion.

NVC's basis is the understanding that our feelings come as a result of our needs and whether they are met or not. As a result of our needs being met, we feel positive feelings like happiness, confidence, and joy. As a result of our needs being unmet, we feel negative feelings like tension, anger and yearning.

There are different types of needs. There are needs such as when you need someone to do something for you like pick up your dry-cleaning. These needs are different than the ones we will discuss here, though. The needs that NVC focuses on are those basic needs that every human has such as connection, peace, meaning, physical well-being, honesty and play. These needs are the same for every human being and are considered to be "basic human needs." One additional and more specific human need that NVC focuses on is the need to contribute to the well-being of other people as well as to contribute to our own well-being. This human need leads us to help others in a genuine way in order to see their well-being improve. This also leads other people to help us by contributing to our well-being. This mutual, genuine helping in order to improve each other's well-being leads others and us to feel the happiness, confidence and joy that is felt when our needs are met.

As I stated, the connection between needs and feelings is the main focus of NVC. In order to understand and practice NVC, it is necessary to gain a better understanding of your feelings and what need they could be connected to. You can then understand if those feelings are a result of the basic human need they are triggered by being met or unmet. Once you understand this, you can better understand the link between other people's feelings and their basic human needs as well. While you are figuring these needs out for yourself, you can ask yourself what you feel and what needs this is in relation to. Some examples of this include feeling delighted because your need for peace is met or feeling annoyed because your need for connection is unmet.

Once you understand all of these things, you can express them to others, and this is the first step in practicing nonviolent communication. You would do so by saying one of the following,

I am feeling ____ because I need ____.

Or

Am I feeling ____ because I need ____?

Or

Are you feeling ____ because you need ____?

More concrete examples of these are below,

I am feeling tension because I need play.

Or

Are you feeling angry because you need honesty?

The Difference Between Violent and Nonviolent Communication

As you now have seen each type of communication on their own, we are going to compare them. Violent communication tends to be the type that we turn to automatically and is the one that is modeled for us when we enter the world as children. On the television, on public transit, and even in our homes growing up, we are exposed to violent communication. It is rare that a person is able to conduct themselves using only nonviolent communication in a world that answers them with violent communication, but it is possible.

Violent communication approaches interactions using negative assumptions and judgments toward other people, and everything that is said comes from these assumptions. When one person approaches an interaction in this way, the other person or people tend to get defensive and they will then also use violent communication. The result is hurt feelings, feelings of inadequacy, feeling judged and shamed, among others. These people who left this interaction feeling these ways then approach their next interaction using violent communication because they are still feeling hurt by their last interaction. The cycle then continues as the hurt feelings and anger are passed from one person to the next over and over again.

On the contrary, when a person approaches an interaction from a place of emotional vulnerability and being open to discovering the other people in the interaction instead of judging them, the other people will tend to respond by also showing emotional vulnerability and genuine concern for the well-being of others. When this is passed on from interaction to interaction instead of violent communication and anger, people leave with positive feelings instead of negative ones.

Changing the interactions that you have with people is not easy, especially if you feel judged or shamed by the words of others. It takes one person in the interaction to be brave enough to approach it in a loving and genuine way to turn it around, and this is how NVC can spread.

In a long-term relationship such as that between spouses or partners, the type of communication you use can have a great impact on the health and longevity of your relationship. Not only in times of conflict but in everyday interactions with your partner, the way that you approach their feelings and their needs creates quite an impact in the long-term. It has been shown that the longevity of a marriage is largely dependent on the ability of the partners to recognize the needs of the other and help them in meeting those needs. This ties into nonviolent communication as it focuses heavily on the needs of people and the feelings that are associated with them. By using compassion and a genuine interest in helping your partner improve their well-being, you will have a healthy and thriving relationship.

The other part of this is the way in which your relationship affects your children. The first relationship that is modeled for a child is the relationship between their parents. By using nonviolent communication with each other, you are modeling a healthy and respectful, a deep and loving relationship. This idea of how a relationship looks is something that your child will take with them into the rest of their life and will form their expectations and ideas of how they will conduct themselves in their own relationship one day. It is important to be mindful of this if you have children.

Learning Nonviolent Communication During Conflicts

Nonviolent communication can be used to resolve many types of conflicts. These problems can be things like deciding who takes your dog for a walk or telling your child to do their homework. While these do not need to be conflicts, sometimes, through the use of violent communication, they can turn into them. By using nonviolent communication, you can stop this before it happens. For example:

If you and your partner are deciding who is going to take your dog for a walk:
"The dog needs to go out for a walk before bed. Having to walk him before bed makes me feel anxious because I have to wake up early in the morning and I need sleep. Would you be willing to take him for his before-bed walk?"

Or:

If you are telling your child to do their homework:
"Your homework has to be done before tomorrow. Seeing you playing video games makes me worried because I value education. Would you be willing to do your homework after dinner before playing more video games?"

Either of these situations has the potential to turn into a much bigger conflict, but by approaching it using nonviolent communication, you can prevent this and even diffuse the situation before it becomes any sort of conflict. Using nonviolent communication for problem solving can be seen as a way to discuss matters in a calm way and can help to make any sort of decision or discuss anything.

When confronted with a conflict, you would want to practice non-violent communication. What nonviolent communication does differently than other methods of conflict resolution or problem solving is that it aims to resolve a situation to the satisfaction of all parties without having to compromise. It aims to promote understanding and compassion instead of the hurt and judgment that is usually a result of confrontation. Nonviolent communication diffuses situations even before they become heated and prevents conflicts altogether. By having everyone express themselves through nonviolent communication, situations are resolved well before anger has built up to the point of an outburst.

Conflict is not an inherently negative or violent thing. It does not have to lead to the breakdown of relationships of any kind or yelling and screaming. It does not have to involve a dominant party and a submissive party or an expresser and a listener.

Conflict can be seen in a positive way in that it can promote voicing one's thoughts and speaking the truth. This is how situations and relationships can be improved rather than harmed.

When using nonviolent communication, you are required to look deep within yourself to examine your feelings and your values. What this does is hold every person accountable for what they are actually feeling instead of having everyone cover up what they are feeling with anger and violence. When you use nonviolent communication, you get used to being able to express your feelings in an articulate and clear manner, which helps in conflict resolution because everyone is then aware of what you need and what you are not getting. This makes the conflict resolution process much simpler as there is no guesswork involved. Sometimes when there is conflict, you must try to discern what the person needs or wants in order to resolve the conflict, but this is quite difficult because only the person themselves can know this. If they express it to you in simple and clear terms, you don't have to spend the time trying to figure out what it is they need and can instead skip right to the point of resolution. This greatly reduces the chances of miscommunications or misunderstandings which can also be a cause of conflicts getting blown out of proportion or feelings of built up resentment.

This type of conflict resolution is not only for co-workers, friends, and family but can also be useful in situations where there is conflict between total strangers or when mediation is required between two people who are in conflict. If you understand nonviolent communication, you can use it for a variety of situations with a variety of people, but the common thread is that it leads to peaceful dialogue. It can help to open lines of communication among people who would not otherwise have peaceful dialogue and creates an understanding between them. It is a powerful tool for any situation that you face.

Nonviolent communication is an effective way to resolve conflicts while ensuring that they do not grow into bigger issues or become large fights that get off topic and end up with both people trying to hurt each other's feelings in any way possible. By using nonviolent communication to resolve conflicts, you are able to stick to the facts of the matter and express yourself in a mature and articulate way. By having steps to stick to loosely, you will be able to resolve any sort of conflict with ease. The great thing about nonviolent communication is that it encourages the other person in the conflict to use it as well. If you approach a conflict using nonviolent communication and the other person begins blaming, shaming, and demanding things from you, you stick to the script of nonviolent communication will show them that they are not using an effective type of communication and they will likely back down quite quickly. By remaining calm and not resorting to blaming, it will be difficult for the other person not to do the same as you are not meeting them with the same level of aggression.

We will now look at some examples of how nonviolent communication can help in conflict resolution.

Example #1:

Your partner leaves his dirty dishes all over the house, and you have been keeping quiet about it, until one day he has friends over for dinner and leaves all of the plates and cutlery in the kitchen dirty and on the table. You come home from work, hungry and tired and want to make yourself some food, but you see that everything in the kitchen is dirty. You feel like you have had enough and finally want to say something. There are two different ways that this confrontation could go.

Method #1: Violent Communication.
"I'm so fed up with the fact that you never do your dishes! I always clean mine but now you have used everything in the kitchen and haven't done your dishes for a week, and everything is dirty! Clean up after yourself; you're a slob. You're lazy and I can't live with it anymore."

Method #2: Nonviolent Communication

I see that all of the dishes and cutlery are dirty since you had people over. Coming home to this state made me feel frustrated because I keep my things clean, and I really value our home being comfortable. Would you be willing to clean a few dishes for me so that I can make dinner?

From the example above, you can see the clear difference in communication styles. In the first method, the person is using judgments and assuming intentions. This would lead their partner to become defensive in response to being called lazy and a slob, and would lead him to respond accordingly. He would likely say something like, "oh yeah, well, you leave the bathroom a mess in the morning and I never say anything, you're the slob!" To which you may drag up another insult that you can think of, and this would go back and forth until both people are exhausted and out of insults and very hurt and angry.

Instead of this, by approaching this frustration using the four steps of nonviolent communication, you are able to state your objective observation of the situation, how it makes you feel and why, and a request for how it can be resolved. To this, your roommate could respond in one of two ways. He could respond by saying, "yes, sure I will do that." Or, "No, I am unable to." The latter may upset you, to which you can ask what he is willing to do to help resolve the situation. In this case, he is much less likely to respond with insults and judgments since he does not feel defensive. Since you approached him in a calm and non-judgmental way, he will likely meet you with the same demeanor. If he does not, you can decide that you have done all that you can and decide for yourself how you will resolve the situation. Maybe you will keep some clean dishes in your room or maybe you will order some takeout that night and try again the next day. Whichever direction this conflict goes, you have avoided becoming involved in a yelling fight where insults are exchanged and feelings are hurt, which is better for you in the end.

Example #2:

You just went on a date, and during the date, you had some trouble finding things to talk about as you and your partner did not have much to say to each other. You are feeling upset because you have been going on many bad dates lately. You are getting frustrated and are considering avoiding dates altogether.

Method #1: Violent Communication
Talking to oneself through inner dialogue: "You are so awkward, and nobody likes awkward people. Why couldn't you think of more things to talk about? They must have hated the date and wanted it to be over!"

Method #2: Nonviolent Communication

Talking to oneself through inner dialogue: "During that date, I ran out of things to talk about. Feeling like there was nothing else to say made me feel uncomfortable because I value connection. Would I be willing to see if I have more in common with the person before I go on a date with them?"

By using nonviolent communication with yourself, you are able to feel better about the situation and focus on what you would like to do the next time instead of making yourself feel ashamed and unworthy. Talking to yourself in a violent way can lead to depression and feelings of negativity toward yourself. It is just as important to use nonviolent communication during inner dialogue as it is to use it when resolving conflicts with others.

Coping With Typical Solvable Problems

As we mentioned throughout this chapter, certain relationship problems don't necessarily need to turn into conflicts. Like the example we used earlier, your partner not doing his dishes doesn't need to turn into a full-blown argument. It can simply be dealt with by problem solving using your nonviolent communication skills. There is a quote that says, 'you have to pick your battles' – this is extremely relevant in this context as there are always going to be problems that arise in life. The difference between it turning into an argument or just a learning lesson is how you decide to deal with it.

If you are faced with a problem from your partner such as he/she not cleaning up after themselves or if they are constantly on their phone during date nights or meal times, it may be as simple as communicating your feelings. However, if you communicate your feelings in a violent manner, these small problems can easily turn into full blown conflicts. Before you let your emotions take over you, take a deep breath, and think about the problem you are struggling with at hand. Is this a serious problem? Can I resolve this problem without starting an argument? Is this something that can easily be changed? Answer those questions in your head and decide what type of communication style you want to use. Remember, you never want to use violent communication unless you can't help it and it happens in the heat of the moment. If you are conscious enough to think straight, it likely isn't a big enough problem and you can utilize nonviolent communication skills to resolve the issue at hand.

The Secret of Restoring Trust

Throughout all relationships, especially long-term ones, there is a high likelihood that you have had a huge argument with your partner that may have shattered your trust for them. This is normal and happens to the best of us. However, if you love this person and want to continue working on a relationship with them, you have to learn to restore trust as mistrust will only lead to more problems. When a person's trust is broken, it often feels as if they can no longer communicate with the other person as they now don't know whether they can be trusted with new information. This is normal. The trick to overcoming this is to force yourself to communicate, even if your thoughts are surrounding the fact that you don't trust them.

The secret to this is all about HOW you communicate this with your partner. Saying phrases such as "I don't trust you anymore!" or "I can never trust you again!" is a form of violent communication and will only cause more distrust in your partner. Instead, communicate your mistrust to your partner in a way that they can emphasize with. For instance, you can say, "That incident has caused me to lose trust in you, it may take us some time to get back to where we were" or "I want to be able to trust you again, but we need some time to work on it." These are all ways where you are letting your partner know that you have lost some trust in them but you have not given up entirely on them.

In addition, it is also important to ask for what you need. If you need your partner to perform certain actions to help you gain the trust back, ask them, and let them know. Don't keep it to yourself. People can't read minds so sitting there silently hoping that your partner will make it up to you somehow will only cause more resentment within yourself. Instead, communicate to them that there may be things they need to do for you in order for the trust to heal. It's all about open communication and the way you deliver your messages. Always use nonviolent communication in situations like this.

Chapter 7: Spice Up Your Sex Life

We are going to be talking about a different topic in this chapter. We spent a lot of time in this book learning about communication and how it can help improve your relationship. Now it's time to take it to a new level and to improve aspects of your sex life as well. This is especially important for those who have been in a relationship with the same person for some time. Things may start to feel a bit dull and sex drives may not be as strong as they used to be. This is the perfect time to start rebuilding that sexual relationship with your partner by trying new things, communicating about personal desires and playing fun games. In this chapter, we will be exploring the following topics; increasing couple intimacy, spicing up your sex life, trying new positions, playing new games and communicating your sexual wants/needs.

Increase Couple Intimacy

As your relationship progresses, it is important to keep sex and lust alive. When you become progressively more and more comfortable with someone, it can take away some of the mystery. This is because there is no longer the excitement of getting to know a person and having everything you do together be brand new. At the beginning of a relationship, you are so eager to have sex with each other because the other person is new and hot and a novelty of sorts. As you get used to them, it can be easy to lose those feelings and settle into the comfortability of everything (like their body or your routine). This is by no means a bad thing. Getting to this point in your relationship is fun and comforting in its own way, and is different from, but in some ways better than, the early stages. From a sexual perspective, though, we don't want the coming of this stage of your relationship to bring with it the end of exciting sex life. This next chapter will teach you how to maintain the lust and intimacy and keep welcoming new sexual adventures together as an established couple.

If you are a long-term or married couple, you have likely tried every one of the classic sex positions together from missionary to 69. You have probably also developed a routine of your favorite positions and the order in which you do them by now. While you probably know how to please each other like it's second nature, rediscovering each other's bodies in a sexy way and learning new ways to pleasure each other is good for couples who have been together for a long time.

At the beginning of a relationship, you may have started having sex casually before you actually got together romantically, or you may have begun having sex when you became a couple. Either way, the beginning of any relationship comes with a lot of uncharted territories. You are exploring a new person's entire body- inside and out, and letting them see all of yours. Of course, this can be nerve-wracking. There will be some positions and sexual activities that you won't be completely comfortable doing with this person yet, even if you have done them before with someone else. There are certain positions you can stick to that are more comfortable at the beginning of a relationship, and that is best for getting to know someone's body and what they like. These positions serve us well when we are newly having sex with a person and are looking for the best way to help each other orgasm. You may think that you are well past this stage in a long-term relationship. This stage of discovery, however, is something that we want to return to every so often. This is because we want to rediscover the person's body and what they like as if it is the first time we are exploring it. People's desires change and their bodies change. It is important to continue to know how to pleasure your partner as they grow and change, and to expect the same from them for yourself. Further, revisiting our partner's body with an open mind as if we know nothing about it can be a fun and flirty way to renew zest in your sex life.

Importance of Spicing Up Your Sex Life

The main importance of spicing up your sex life is to increase intimacy between you and your partner. Not only does this help your sex life become more fun and exciting, but it also improves the communication and bond between you and your partner. In this chapter, we will be examining intimacy and the role that it plays in romantic relationships. We are going to look at how you can work to maintain intimacy with your partner and what achieving a greater level of intimacy can and will do for your relationship.

Intimacy is very important between two people when part of a couple, especially in the bedroom. Intimacy is what brings you close and keeps you close. Firstly, we will look at what intimacy means and the different types of intimacy that exist. There are different types of intimacy, and here I will outline them for you before digging deeper into the intimacy that exists between couples. Intimacy, in a general sense, is defined as mutual openness and vulnerability between two people. There are different ways in which you can give and receive openness and vulnerability in a relationship. Intimacy does not have to include a sexual relationship (though it can). Therefore, it is not only reserved for romantic relationships. Intimacy can also be present in other types of close relationships like friendships or family relationships. Below, I will outline the different forms of intimacy.

Emotional Intimacy

Emotional intimacy is the ability to express oneself in a mature and open manner, leading to a deep emotional connection between people. Saying things like "I love you" or "you are very important to me" are examples of this. It is also the ability to respond in a mature and open way when someone expresses themselves to you by saying things like "I'm sorry" or "I love you too." This type of open and vulnerable dialogue leads to an emotional connection. In order for a deep emotional connection to form, there must be a mutual willingness to be vulnerable and open with one's deeper thoughts and feelings. This is where this type of emotional intimacy comes from.

Intellectual Intimacy

Intellectual intimacy is a kind of intimacy that involves discussing and sharing thoughts and opinions on intellectual matters, from which they gain fulfillment and feelings of closeness with the other person. For example, if you are discussing politics with someone who you deem to be an intellectual equal, you may find that you feel a closeness with them as you share your thoughts and opinions and connect on an intellectual level. Many people find intellect and brains to be sexy in a partner!

Shared Interests and Activities

This form of intimacy is less well-known, but it is also considered a form of intimacy. When you share activities with another person that you both enjoy and are passionate about, this creates a sense of connection. For example, when you cook together or travel together. These shared experiences give you memories to share and this leads to bonding and intimacy (openness and vulnerability). This type of connection is usually present in friendships, in familial relationships and more importantly, in romantic relationships. Being able to share interests and activities leads to a closeness that can be defined as intimacy.

Physical Intimacy

Physical intimacy is the type that most people think of when they hear the term "intimacy," and it is the kind that we will be most concerned within this book, as it is the type of intimacy that includes sex and all activities related to sex. It also involves other non-sexual types of physical contact such as hugging and kissing. Physical intimacy can be found in close friendships or familial relationships where hugging and kisses on the cheek are common, but it is most often found in romantic relationships.

Physical intimacy is the type of intimacy involved when people are trying to make each other orgasm. Physical intimacy is almost always required for orgasm. Physical intimacy doesn't necessarily mean that you are in love with the person you are having sex with; it just means that you are doing something intimate with another person in a physical way.

It is also possible to be intimate with yourself, and while this begins with the emotional intimacy of self-awareness, it also involves the physical intimacy of masturbation and physical self-exploration. I define sexual, physical intimacy of the self as being in touch with the parts of yourself physically that you would not normally be in touch with. If you are a woman, your breasts, your clitoris, your vagina and your anus. If you are a man, your testicles, your penis, your anus. Being able to be physically intimate with yourself allows you to have more fulfilling sex, more fulfilling orgasms and a more fulfilling overall relationship with your body. We will discuss this in more detail later on in this book. Allowing someone to be physically intimate with you in a sexual way is also an emotionally intimate experience, regardless of your relationship with the person. Being in charge of your own body while it is in the hands of another person is very important and this is why masturbation is such a key element to physical intimacy.

You can think of physical intimacy as something that breaks the barrier of personal space. By this definition, this includes touching of any sort, but especially sexual intercourse, kissing touching, and anything else of a sexual nature. When you are having sex with anyone, regardless of whether you have romantic feelings for them or not, you are having a physically intimate relationship with them. The difference between a relationship that involves physical intimacy alone and no other forms of intimacy and a romantic relationship is that a romantic relationship will also involve emotional intimacy, shared activities and intellectual intimacy is that a deep and lasting romantic relationship will need to include all of these forms of intimacy at once.

New Positions to Try

When it comes to sex, changing the positions you use is the key to keeping it interesting and different. After a short time, a sexual routine can become boring and old, because you know what to expect at every turn and what to do next without thinking at all. Your brain, heart, and body do not need to be engaged like they are when you are doing something new and exciting that is really turning you on. When you are performing a sex position that you have never tried before, your entire body is engaged, thinking about what is next, feeling new sensations, looking to the other person to see if they are feeling pleasure as well. This is very different from performing a position you have done many times over. This is why changing your sex positions is beneficial; it engages every part of you. In this chapter, I will be teaching you about a few new positions that you and your partner can try in order to spice things up a bit!

Standing Suspended

This position requires strength from the man but can lead to very deep penetration if he is able to support his woman's weight enough. This position will be a workout for him, but a workout with a better ending than any workout he'll have in the gym!

The man stands facing the wall, and the woman stands in front of him, facing him. She puts her arms around his neck and jumps into his arms (how movie moment-esque). He supports her weight by holding onto her butt cheeks while she has her arms and legs wrapped around him. He holds her up like this and lifts her higher to lower her onto his erect penis. Once inside, he can pin her against the wall for support so that he doesn't have to support her weight entirely and can use his hands to move her up and down on his hard member. If her back is supported by the wall, the man can also thrust into her using his hips if his arms get too tired. Because of the angle, the woman's legs are held at, her vagina and legs are open enough so that the man can penetrate her very deeply. This is one of the best positions if you want to attain very deep penetration. This increases the chances of the woman's G-spot being hit and will allow her to reach a G-spot orgasm that will drive her crazy!

The Waterfall

The waterfall is a position that can bring something new to your bedroom routine. This position requires some flexibility and strength from both people but holds lots of pleasure potential.

The man will begin by sitting in a chair with his feet on the floor. The woman will climb onto his lap and insert his penis into her.

She can wrap her legs around his waist. Then, slowly she will lean all the way back until her head and arms are touching the floor (with pillows underneath). From here, the man will hold onto her hips and can move her body onto his penis at whatever speed and depth he wishes. He can also grab onto her breasts and massage her clitoris in this position if he wishes.

The Scissors

This position is a little difficult to get yourselves into, but once you do, it will be well worth the effort. To begin, the man will sit on the bed with his arms behind him, holding his weight up but leaning back. Then, he will bend one of his knees, so his leg is bent. The woman will lie down on the bed face-down and with her head at the opposite end of the bed as the man's. She will spread her legs and move her body toward the man's until their bodies meet. When they meet, their bodies will look like two pairs of scissors crossed into one another. From here, the man will insert his penis into her vagina. The woman can move her body up and down on his penis, and the man can thrust into her. It may take a bit of time to develop a rhythm in this position, but when you do, you will both feel intense pleasure.

The Wheelbarrow

This position got its name because the positioning of both of your bodies makes it so that you look like a person pushing a wheelbarrow. To get into position, the girl will get into a downward dog position. If you aren't sure what that is, it is a yoga position where you have your arms outstretched and your hands planted on the floor, and your buttocks in the air with your legs straight and your toes on the floor. Get into a downward dog, but spread your legs slightly. The man then stands between the woman's legs and will hold onto her hips. From here, he will lift her hips and hold her legs in the air while her hands remain planted on the ground. She will stick her legs straight out past him. He can now insert his penis into her vagina.

This position is quite involved and may be difficult to get into, but it allows for lots of movement control by both people as the woman can move her hips up or down to adjust the angle, the man can thrust himself into her or pull her hips towards his penis and can also change the angle of his hips. All of this customization potential makes it so that there is a lot of room for change to ensure that both people are receiving as much pleasure as possible.

The Rowing Boat

The rowing boat is another position that you may never have heard of, but that will make for an exciting new sexual experience for you and your partner. This one begins with the man sitting on the floor or the bed with his knees bent and his legs spread. The woman will sit in exactly the same way, except she will be facing him. She will move her body toward him and when they come as close as they can to one another, she will slide her knees underneath his knees, so that her legs are still bent, but underneath his. Her legs will then be holding his legs apart and open, and he will hold onto her legs to hold them open and bent. Then, he will slide his penis into her and they can grind together for penetration to occur. This is an intimate position as you can both see each other's faces and are sitting with your legs spread right in front of each other. It is also intimate because it involves both people coming together with their bodies vulnerable and completely exposed and their entirety open to their partner. This vulnerability will bring you both closer together and this will lead to greater levels of intimacy and connection, especially since you will be able to see each other the entire time.

The Maid

This position is great for giving the woman blended or multiple orgasms of any sort, and this position is spicy because it incorporates a little bit of role play. This position is done on a ledge or a countertop, or even on the washing machine. Take this one to the kitchen for a nice change of scenery. The woman can even wear an apron with nothing else underneath to add a bit of a sexy role play element to this one if she wishes. The woman sits on the countertop with her legs spread, and her man stands in between her legs. She wraps her legs around him. He enters her from the front and will easily be able to hit her G-Spot in this position because of the angle of penetration. Having the woman sitting upright is a good way to ensure G-Spot contact. While he is hitting her G-Spot over and over, the pleasure will continue to build until she reaches an internal orgasm. If he continues to penetrate her in the exact same way at a steady rhythm, she will be able to keep feeling pleasure and keep having G-Spot orgasms over and over again. If she wants to try for a blended orgasm in this position, she can lean her upper body back against the cabinet and touch her clitoris as he is thrusting into her. This will lead to both a clitoral and G-Spot orgasm at the same time and this means double the pleasure. He can continue to thrust into her even after this blended orgasm and she can then wrap her arms around his neck while he penetrates her without clitoral stimulation, and she will then have multiple vaginal orgasms after this. He will have to try hard to hold off his orgasm throughout all of this as he will be very turned on by all of the pleasure his woman is feeling from his penis.

Games to Play

In this subchapter, we will look at ways to spice up your sex life with some fun games and challenges you can play, of the erotic variety, of course. Including sexy games and challenges will keep your relationship fun and flirtatious for a long time to come and these you can keep changing and introducing new ones to keep the experimentation alive. You may have played innocently flirtatious games in middle school like spin the bottle or 7 minutes in heaven. We are going to use a similar idea of fun and games but a *much* less innocent variety. These games are designed for you and your partner to have some sexy fun together. You can use this as foreplay or as fun in the evening. It doesn't have to progress to full-blown sex, but I assure you that you both will be heavily turned on after playing one of these that you will not be able to wait to get to penetration. Just try not to come too early on in the game!

Never Have I Ever

This game is a fun way to learn more about your partner's sexual history, but in turn, they will also learn about yours! Both of you will begin with five fingers up- these represent your lives. One of you goes first and says something they have never done, for example: "Never have I ever had a threesome." If your partner has done it, they have to put down one finger. You go back and forth like this and the first person to lose all of their lives loses the game! The loser will then have to give the winner something of their choosing. This game can also be played as a drinking game where, instead of lives using fingers, if the other person has done the thing you say, they have to take a sip of their drink. If you play this way, it can go on for quite a while since there are no lives. To keep it fun and lighthearted, say things that you have not done, but that is not targeted at the other person such as "never have I ever been named John" if your partner is named John. Keep it fun and sexy by saying things related to dating, sex and all taboo topics you can think of. Play this game with the intention of getting to know your partner better and having them get to know you better as well.

Spin the Bottle

Traditional spin the bottle is done in a large group of people, with each person being an option the bottle can land on. Everyone sits in a circle with the bottle lying on its side in the middle. You spin the bottle on its side and whoever the opening is facing when it stops spinning is the person that you have to kiss.

In this spin on spin the bottle, we are going to switch it up a little bit. You can play this game with anything you have, all you'll need is some type of bottle, some paper, and a pen. Think of the regular spin the bottle circle, with 6 or 8 people all sitting in a circle. Instead of people, we are going to have one challenge at each spot. At each spot, there will be a piece of paper with a challenge written on it, and whichever spot the bottleneck is facing after your spin

Lick my nipples

Give me a hickey

Give me oral sex for 2 minutes

Pick which position we will have sex in after this game

Strip down to your underwear

Give me a massage on a body part of my choosing for 2 minutes

Give me a lap dance

Take off my shirt using your teeth

I will look for the craziest sex position I can find online, and you attempt it with me

Truth or Dare

Play sexy Truth or Dare with your partner. Just like when you were young, a game of Truth or Dare helps you get to know people in a funny and sometimes daring way. If you don't know how to play, I will explain the rules first! Each partner takes a turn asking the other person, "Truth or Dare?" The person responds with their answer, and depending on which they choose, a truth- a question that they have to answer truthfully, or a dare- a challenge that they have to complete, is given to them. If they do not complete the dare or will not answer the truth question, they have to accept a pre-determined punishment. This punishment can be to take a shot (If you are playing a drinking version) or to give you a massage, anything you wish. Decide this punishment at the beginning of the game. As you play, you will make up truths or dares for your partner that get them to tell you or do things to you that are fun and sexy! Below are some examples of truths or dares that you can give them:

Truths:
Tell me your wildest sexual fantasy
What did you think about/imagine/ watch last time you masturbated?
What is your favorite sexual memory?
What is something you have always wanted to try during sex?

What is the naughtiest thing you have ever done?

Dares:

Lick peanut butter off of somewhere on your body of your choosing ex. finger, chest

Turn the lights off and try to turn the other person on using only sounds

Do a striptease to a song of your choosing

Make out with their belly button

Demonstrate their favorite sex position with a pillow

Give them a lap dance

Give them a hickey

How to Communicate Your Sexual Needs

Communicating your sexual needs may be a difficult and embarrassing task, especially if you want to do something that is deemed as 'kinky' or a 'fetish.' Just like in strong and healthy relationships, communication is key. This goes the same for sexual relationships with your partner. If you have a kink or a fetish that you want your partner to try with you, you have to learn how to communicate it to them.

You may be self-conscious about what turns you on and unsure of how your partner will feel about it. If you have been in this relationship for a while now and you still have not discussed these with your partner, your anxiety about bringing them up has likely only increased with time. At the beginning of a relationship, you may be hesitant to bring up things that please you that you deem unusual or not-so-vanilla. This is completely understandable, and we will discuss how to bring these topics up in conversation, regardless of how long you have been in your current relationship or marriage. The other reason could be that you have just recently discovered a new kink, and that is okay as well. Read on to find out how and when to best explore this with your partner.

Before we begin, keep in mind that many of us think our kinks are odd and embarrassing, but they are probably not as off the wall as you think they are. Fetishes may also be embarrassing to discuss, but if you are so into a certain thing that you require it in order to be pleased, your partner will surely be interested. As your partner, they are invested in your pleasure and should always be wondering how best to please you. So how do you initiate a conversation about your kinks or fetishes with your partner or spouse? The key is entering the conversation with the intention of not only explaining to them your own desires but of listening to and understanding your partner's kinks and fetishes as well.

Begin by asking your partner if there is anything that they have been interested in trying in the bedroom, or if there is anything new that they have wanted to explore sexually with you. This will initiate an open dialogue about sex and desires in general. Listen with an open mind; your partner may be into something that you are also into! Next, they will likely ask you the same question back. Explain to them that you have wanted to try something new in your sex life with them. Explain to them what it is and how it makes you feel. Maybe you have explored this in a past relationship and maybe that is where you first discovered this specific thing that turns you on. Maybe you have never tried it with someone else and you would like to begin exploring it with them. If this person loves you, they care about your pleasure. Even if they may have reservations about trying something new, they are likely to be open to giving it a shot for you. Be open to exploring your kink or fetish at a beginner level if your partner has never tried it before. Sex is all about comfort and pleasure and as long as you are both feeling these two things, preferably by meeting in the middle, a good time is sure to be had by all. When explaining your kink to them, be sure to explain how it makes you feel and how it could make them feel. Explain what exactly you enjoy about it. Explain how exactly you enjoy it and what role you like to take in it. Do you like to be the dominant one? The submissive one? Allow them to ask questions and be curious. the ability to have an open conversation about sex in a relationship is essential to having a positively evolving sex life as your relationship grows and progresses. You want your sex life to grow and change along with the both of you.

We will now look at a couple of examples of this and how this conversation may go for you, in order for you to feel more secure when bringing this up.

As an example, say your kink is rough sex. You and your partner may have been having soft, gentle, and loving sex up until this point because you know that that is what they like, but you have learned through a past relationship that you love rough sex. You may not have tried this or brought it up in conversation before because you were afraid that your partner would have been turned off or afraid. In order to bring this up to them in conversation, you can begin by saying something like, "I used to get very turned on by having rough sex, and I would like to try it with you." There are many degrees of roughness in sex and it will be easy to start out by just dipping your toes in the world of rough sex to see how your partner feels about it. You can explain this to them as well. Once they are comfortable with the idea and are wanting to try it with you, you will need to take the lead. Your partner will probably not know where to start and you will lead them through it for their first few times. To teach them as you go, try using dirty talk to make it sexier than if you just gave them a lesson in kink like a lecture at school. Begin by explaining to them whether you enjoy being in the position of masochist (pleasure from pain inflicted on you) or sadist (pleasure from inflicting pain on another person). For example, you may like having your hair pulled or having your partner dig their nails into your back when you make them feel good.

Begin by having sex as you usually would, and when it comes time that you would like it to get a little rougher, tell your partner (using dirty talk) what you want them to do. Say something like the following; "pull my hair baby" or "spank me like you're punishing me." This will make your directions sexy and fitting for the mood. Your partner may be afraid to hurt you if they do not have experience with rough sex. You can assure them before you begin that they will not be hurting you but in fact, they will be making you feel more pleasure than usual. They will likely be excited by this possibility.

Conclusion

First of all, I'd like you to give yourself a pat on the back for your hard work in finishing this book. It is not easy to take a look at yourself, identify problem areas and learn how to fix them for the sake of your relationship. This takes hard work and should not be underestimated. A part of continuously improving your relationship is to help you and your partner build a secure future together. This doesn't mean that exercising some of the strategies learned in this book is going to secure a future with you and your partner. The only way to do that is to continue practicing these strategies and principles even in the hardest of times. The only thing more important than communication with one another is commitment to each other.

Remember, you may feel like you are filled to the brim of new knowledge right now. However, the only way to actually see positive results is so to apply the things you've learned into your daily life. You don't necessarily have to start with your partner but you can simply start using some new strategies you've learned on friends, acquaintances or coworkers. Building healthy habits of communication with everyone you come across will ensure that you are also doing this consistently with your partner. The more you practice open communication and healthy habits, the easier it will be to navigate the relationship with you and your partner and have them practice the same healthy methods as well.

So, what's next after this? To tell you the truth, it's simply commitment and communication. Always remember that over communicating is better than under communicating, and all issues and conflicts can be resolved simply by having effective communication through the use of nonviolent strategies. Whatever life throws at you and your partner, talk about it. Work as a team. The best way to overcome the obstacles that come up in life is to have a trusty partner in crime to do it with.

Made in the USA
Monee, IL
29 March 2021